AF271364

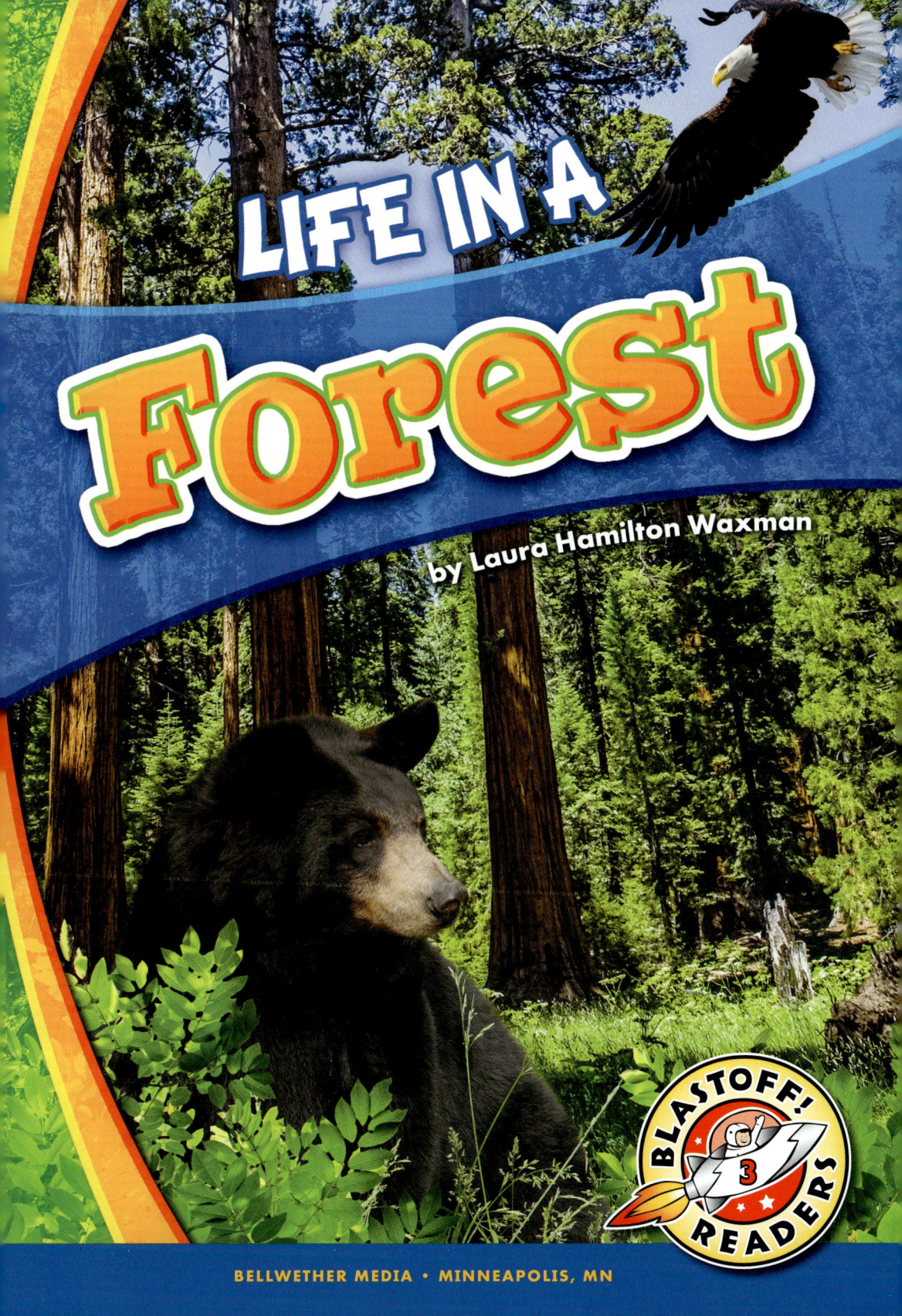

LIFE IN A Forest

by Laura Hamilton Waxman

BELLWETHER MEDIA • MINNEAPOLIS, MN

BLASTOFF! READERS

3

Note to Librarians, Teachers, and Parents:

Blastoff! Readers are carefully developed by literacy experts and combine standards-based content with developmentally appropriate text.

Level 1 provides the most support through repetition of high-frequency words, light text, predictable sentence patterns, and strong visual support.

Level 2 offers early readers a bit more challenge through varied simple sentences, increased text load, and less repetition of high-frequency words.

Level 3 advances early-fluent readers toward fluency through increased text and concept load, less reliance on visuals, longer sentences, and more literary language.

Level 4 builds reading stamina by providing more text per page, increased use of punctuation, greater variation in sentence patterns, and increasingly challenging vocabulary.

Level 5 encourages children to move from "learning to read" to "reading to learn" by providing even more text, varied writing styles, and less familiar topics.

Whichever book is right for your reader, Blastoff! Readers are the perfect books to build confidence and encourage a love of reading that will last a lifetime!

This edition first published in 2016 by Bellwether Media, Inc.

No part of this publication may be reproduced in whole or in part without written permission of the publisher. For information regarding permission, write to Bellwether Media, Inc., Attention: Permissions Department, 5357 Penn Avenue South, Minneapolis, MN 55419.

Library of Congress Cataloging-in-Publication Data

Waxman, Laura Hamilton, author.
  Life in a Forest / by Laura Hamilton Waxman.
    pages cm. – (Blastoff! Readers. Biomes Alive!)
  Summary: "Simple text and full-color photography introduce beginning readers to life in a forest. Developed by literacy experts for students in kindergarten through third grade"– Provided by publisher.
  Audience: Ages 5-8.
  Audience: K to grade 3.
  Includes bibliographical references and index.
  ISBN 978-1-62617-317-0 (hardcover : alk. paper)
  1. Forest ecology–Juvenile literature. 2. Forest animals–Juvenile literature. 3. Forest plants–Juvenile literature. 4. Forests and forestry–Climatic factors–Juvenile literature. I. Title.
  QH541.5.F6W39 2016
  577.3–dc23
                    2015030698

Printed in the United States of America, North Mankato, MN.

Table of Contents

The Forest Biome

Forests cover one-third of the earth. They make up the largest land **biome** on the planet!

Trees of different types fill these shady places. Some lose their leaves. Others keep their leaves year-round.

maple tree

Very different areas can have forests. Closest to the **equator** are **tropical** forests. **Temperate** forests lie farther north and south. **Boreal** forests are just below the **Arctic**.

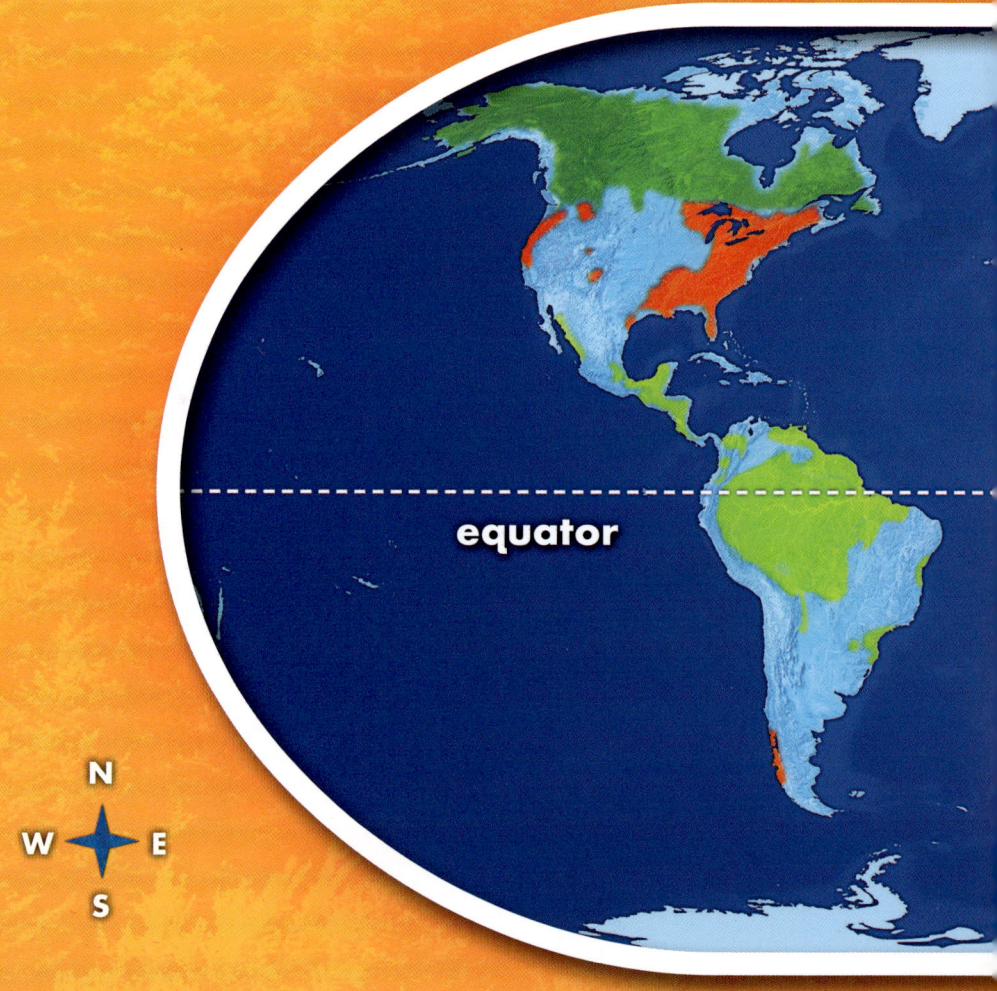

equator

N
W E
S

Forests grow in both low and high places. Some rise from steep mountainsides.

tropical forests =

temperate forests =

boreal forests =

The Climate

Finland boreal forest

A forest's **climate** depends on its location. Boreal forests stay extremely cold most of the year. Snow blankets trees during the long winter.

Tropical forests stay warm and wet. Some receive up to 400 inches (1,016 centimeters) of rain in one year!

Borneo rain forest

summer

Temperate forests have four seasons. Temperatures and **precipitation** change with every season.

These forests warm to around 70 degrees Fahrenheit (21 degrees Celsius) in summer. During winter, temperatures often drop below **freezing**.

The Plants

canopy

A forest is made of layers of plants. The tallest trees form the top **canopy**.

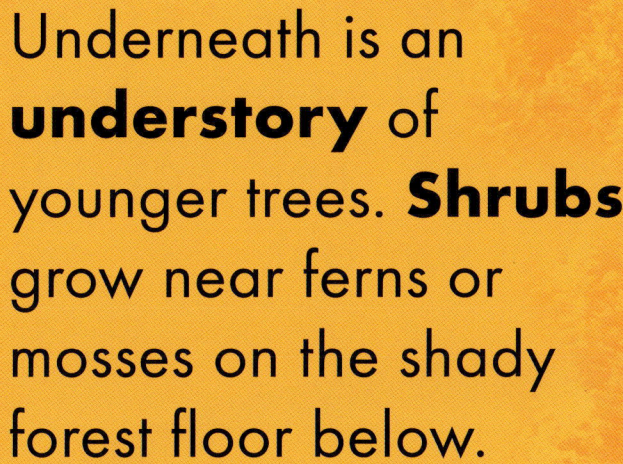

Underneath is an **understory** of younger trees. **Shrubs** grow near ferns or mosses on the shady forest floor below.

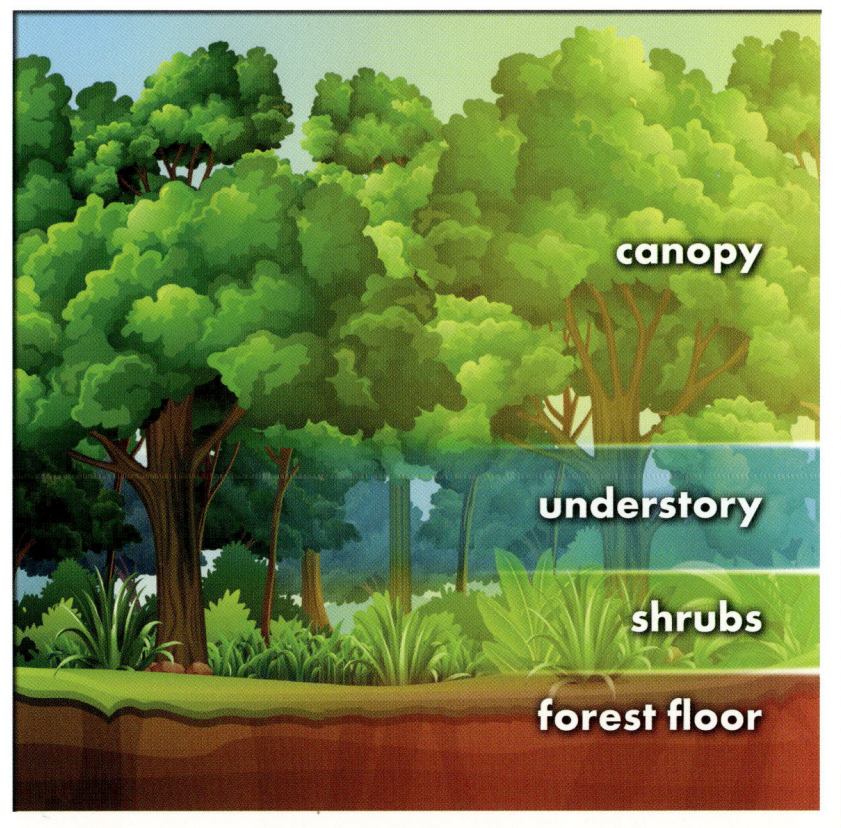

canopy

understory

shrubs

forest floor

The tallest trees take up the most space. Their branches stretch way out. Their leaves take in a lot of sunlight.

Shorter trees and shrubs have bigger leaves than canopy trees. This helps them soak in the little sunlight that gets through.

flying squirrel

Many forest animals are good climbers or fliers. They use trees for homes, hiding places, and food.

16

Some small forest animals are strong diggers. They have sharp claws to make underground homes and to get dinner.

mole

Eurasian jay

bald eagle

Forests are full of birds. The shapes of their beaks tell what they eat. Thick beaks with pointed tips crack nuts and seeds. Sharp, hooked beaks grasp small animals.

Some birds must survive cold winters. Many others **migrate** to warmer places where there is plenty to eat!

downy woodpecker

broad-winged hawks migrating

The Redwood Forests

Location: northern California, United States

Size of Redwood National and State Parks: 206 square miles (534 square kilometers)

Forest type: temperate

Temperature: 45 °F to 60 °F (7 °C to 16 °C)

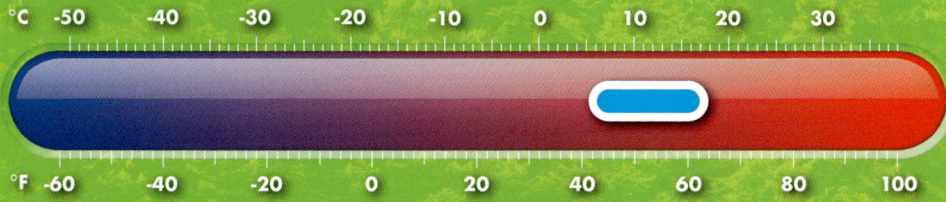

Precipitation: 70 inches (178 centimeters) per year

REDWOOD FOREST FOOD WEB

bald eagle

raccoon

coast redwood tree

banana slug

mountain lion

huckleberries

western gray squirrel

Other important plants: Douglas firs, redwood sorrels, ferns, lilies, yarrow flowers

Other important animals: Steller's jays, chickadees, hummingbirds, swifts, chipmunks, elk, deer, black bears, coyotes

Glossary

Arctic—the cold region around the North Pole

biome—a nature community defined by its climate, land features, and living things

boreal—located in northern areas

canopy—the top layer of a forest; the tallest trees in a forest form the canopy.

climate—the specific weather conditions for an area

equator—the imaginary line that divides Earth into northern and southern halves

freezing—32 degrees Fahrenheit (0 degrees Celsius); the temperature at which water freezes into ice.

migrate—to travel from one place to another, often with the seasons

precipitation—water that falls to the earth from the sky

shrubs—short, woody plants

temperate—mild; not too hot or too cold.

tropical—relating to the tropics, a hot region near the equator

understory—the layer of a forest below the canopy and above the forest floor

To Learn More

AT THE LIBRARY

Fleisher, Paul. *Forest Food Webs in Action*. Minneapolis, Minn.: Lerner Publications Co., 2014.

Ringstad, Arnold. *Forest Habitats*. Mankato, Minn.: Child's World, 2014.

Slade, Suzanne. *What If There Were No Gray Wolves? A Book About the Temperate Forest Ecosystem*. Mankato, Minn.: Picture Window Books, 2011.

ON THE WEB

Learning more about forests is as easy as 1, 2, 3.

1. Go to www.factsurfer.com.

2. Enter "forests" into the search box.

3. Click the "Surf" button and you will see a list of related web sites.

With factsurfer.com, finding more information is just a click away.

Index